vodka

discovering, exploring, enjoying

vodka

discovering, exploring, enjoying

RYLAND
PETERS
& SMALL

LONDON NEW YORK

ian wisniewski

photography by **william lingwood**

Designer Luis Peral-Aranda
Editor Miriam Hyslop
Location Research Claire Hector
Picture Research Emily Westlake
Production Deborah Wehner
Art Director Gabriella Le Grazie
Publishing Director Alison Starling

Food Stylist Joss Herd
Cocktail recipes Tony Conigliaro

First published in the United States in 2003
by Ryland Peters & Small, Inc.
519 Broadway
5th Floor
New York NY10012
www.rylandpeters.com

10 9 8 7 6 5 4 3 2 1

Text © Ian Wisniewski 2003
Design and photographs
© Ryland Peters & Small 2003

ISBN 1 84172 506 4

Library of Congress Cataloging-in-Publication data
is available on request.

Printed and bound in China

contents

where it's at   6

how it's made   14

where it's made   22

enjoying vodka   48

credits   62

index   63

acknowledgments   64

The world's most popular liquor, vodka is perfect for every drinking opportunity—sipped neat, shot down in one, or savored in a delicious cocktail. And as the choice of vodkas from around the world becomes ever more varied, including flavored and deluxe styles, interest in this fascinating drink continues to grow. The result is a dedicated vodka-lovers' fraternity, continually scanning bar shelves for something new.

where it's at

cocktail culture

Vodka's ability to mix with a wider range of ingredients than any other hard liquor means it has developed an unrivaled repertoire of cocktails. And as cocktails have become an essential element of contemporary lifestyles, the future for vodka has never looked better.

Dominating every bar list, vodka has inspired the most fashionable new creations, like the Cosmopolitan and the Sea Breeze. Meanwhile, classics such as the Moscow Mule and Harvey Wallbanger are being rediscovered, and reordered, by a new generation of the cocktail brigade.

Another recent triumph is that vodka has largely replaced gin as the liquor of choice in the Dry Martini. Always the world's ultimate cocktail, the Dry Martini has a sophisticated allure that other cocktails can only dream of.

The choice of vodka cocktails—which are a perfect introduction to the alcohol, before trying it neat—ranges from fruity and creamy to spicy and savory styles. Such a comprehensive selection ensures there is a cocktail to suit every taste, as well as every mood and occasion. This also means it's easy to overindulge, and suffer the consequences! But even then, vodka can provide a remedy with that classic hangover cure, the Bloody Mary.

style icon

An international success story, vodka has transcended the usual cycle that sees different hard liquors go in and out of fashion virtually every decade. Vodka has also become a self-perpetuating phenomenon. As the range of brands and styles continues to grow, interest in vodka deepens, encouraging distillers to add to the throng.

Alcohol brands, like our choice of clothing or car, have become a lifestyle issue that defines us. It's a case of "you are what you drink," or at least what you are seen to be ordering. But unlike the conspicuous consumption of the 1980s, when mere spending power displayed status, the current agenda is a desire for quality and individuality. It's about being a connoisseur who deserves the best, and is fully equipped to appreciate a vodka's finer points.

A growing audience is now eager to discover the differences between the array of brands, so they can make informed choices. In such a competitive environment, it's essential for a vodka to establish individuality, with "the look" an obvious starting point. The result is that sophisticated, innovative design has produced an amazing range of bottles, and bar shelves increasingly resemble catwalks.

Technical details of the production process are often promoted to help establish a brand's identity. Consequently, the traditional advertising message that suggests "drink me, and you, too, will be fashionable and fabulous" is changing. Brands now entice us with an alternative suggestion: "Drink me, I'm different—and that will make you different too."

the flavor factor

While vodka's allure continues to flourish, there are still those who assume that all vodkas taste the same. There is a logical explanation for this view in certain countries, as the traditional style of vodka produced in the U.K. and U.S.A. is "neutral." As the term suggests, neutral vodka has no discernible aroma or flavor, with all trace of the grain from which it is distilled being removed.

In vodka's homelands of Poland, Russia, Sweden, and Finland, the approach has always been entirely different, with the spirit retaining the character of the grain. The choice of grain varies, with wheat used in Sweden and Russia, barley in Finland, and rye in Poland.

Vodkas distilled from each type of grain show readily discernible differences. Anise flavors, for example, are classic in a wheat vodka such as Altai, while rye vodkas like Wyborowa and Potocki yield mellow, nutty rye notes with subtle sweetness. Finlandia exemplifies the character of barley, with lightly nutty, ripe grain notes balanced by a hint of luscious spice.

Of course, even vodkas distilled from the same grain offer plenty of individuality. Comparing Russian wheat vodkas reveals Altai to have savory, anise notes balanced by creamy hints of vanilla and citrus, while Russky Standart delivers a focused, rounded anise and licorice medley.

Blending different grains extends the range of flavor even further. Grey Goose is a multi-grain triumph that resembles vodka's greatest hits, combining rye, wheat, barley, and corn (a traditional ingredient of American vodkas).

Being French, Grey Goose also exemplifies another recent phenomenon. The traditional division between Eastern European and Scandinavian

vodkas offering character, compared to a neutral Western style, no longer applies. In fact, a host of new wave brands from countries without an indigenous vodka tradition, such as Ketel One from the Netherlands, offer abundant character. They are also contributing to the evolution of contemporary vodka.

While clear (i.e. unflavored) vodka accounts for the vast majority of the market, the popularity and range of flavored styles continues to grow. Lemon is currently the world's favorite flavor, with brands such as Cytrynowka and Wyborowa Lemon from Poland, and Limonnaya from Russia, each offering an individual character. In fact, a citrus contingent has evolved, including Danzka Grapefruit, Grey Goose L'Orange, and Ketel One Citroen. The fruit theme continues with a choice of cherry, apple, plum, peach, pineapple, melon, and berry-flavored vodkas such

as black currant and raspberry. There's even a vegetable in the form of Polstar Cucumber vodka.

Krupnik (honey vodka), Stolichnaya Kafka (coffee), and Kremlyovskaya Chocolate satisfy another range of favorite tastes. Similarly, herbs and spices find an ultimate incarnation in brands such as Pieprzowka and Pertsovka (pepper), as well as *digestif* styles like Zoladkowa Gorzka and Zoladkowka.

One of the most historic vodkas is Zubrowka, dating from the 16th century. This is flavored with a wild herb, bison grass, which grows in eastern Poland's Bialowieza Forest, a national park where wild bison still roam. Once dried, the grass is infused in the spirit, yielding a complex, rewarding vodka. Herbaceous, lavender, jasmine tea, and citrus flavors open up further with hints of vanilla, tobacco, chocolate, and caffè latte. Sensational.

Each stage of the production process influences a vodka's character, including the choice of grain, the method of distillation, the type of water used, and the distillers' own style. Meanwhile, the scale of production varies enormously. Major international brands are produced at a phenomenal rate while specialist producers have a more "hands-on" approach right down to sticking the labels on the bottles.

VODKA

(80 PROOF)

"Superluxe" by the Kryshtal Minsk
Amalgamation Factory founded in 1893
DISTILLED FROM WHEAT

how it's made

ingredients

Most vodkas are produced from grain, and the type of grain used is the most influential factor in the resulting flavor. The choice of wheat, rye, barley, or corn is essentially a practical one, depending on the grain cultivated in each country. This explains why so many Polish vodkas are produced from rye, while Finlandia is produced at the Koskenkorva distillery in southern Finland, the country's best terrain for barley. Similarly, Absolut is distilled at Ahus in southern Sweden, using wheat grown in the surrounding province of Skane.

Wheat vodka is distilled from winter wheat, which is sown in the autumn and harvested the following autumn. However, in Siberia, winter wheat has to endure long winters and make the most of brief summers. Seeds sprout and mature in three months, ready to be harvested in July. Similarly, in Finland, barley is sown in May and harvested in mid-August. The summer sun compensates for such a tight schedule by barely setting, providing more than 20 hours of light daily.

Potatoes are also a traditional ingredient for vodka, used in Poland since the 18th century as well as in Norway, Estonia, and the U.S.A. Although it is typically assumed that grain vodkas are superior, potato vodkas can also offer supreme quality; they just have a different character. In Poland only special potato varieties are used for distillation, cultivated in specific areas of central Poland and the Baltic coast.

While individual grains and potatoes offer a spectrum of flavors, the choice of ingredient also entails technical differences. The yield of alcohol, for example, depends on the level of starch within each ingredient (more starch means more alcohol). As this varies significantly among ingredients, it's an important factor, which also influences the cost of production. Corn leads the hierarchy, followed by wheat, rye, and barley, with potatoes giving the lowest yield.

distilling the spirit

Before grain can be distilled it needs to be milled (crushed), and cooked in hot water. Cooking releases the all-important starch content in the grain, and together with the addition of enzymes this also converts the starch into sugars. The resulting liquid is fermented by adding yeast, which converts the sugars into alcohol. Known as the "wash," this liquid has an alcoholic strength of 8–10% a.b.v. (alcohol by volume) or 16–20 proof. The remaining 90% or so is water.

The process of distillation separates the alcohol from the water, by heating the wash in a "still" (an enclosed vessel). Since alcohol evaporates at a lower temperature than water, heating the wash causes the alcohol to vaporize, and rise up the full height of the still. These vapors can then be collected and cooled, when they will condense into alcohol. The more the wash is distilled, the higher the strength of the resulting spirit, and the purer the alcohol.

There are two methods used, the most historic being pot still distillation. A pot still resembles a large kettle, and can only distil alcohol in batches. This means it takes longer than continuous distillation, a more modern method that enables spirit to be produced nonstop. Continuous stills typically comprise around three to five linked columns, with each column removing a different range of impurities from the alcoholic vapors. After passing through the final column, vapors are condensed and collected as alcohol.

Distilling the wash produces spirit with an alcoholic strength of up to 96% a.b.v. (192 proof),

which is then diluted with water to reach the usual bottling strength. This varies among brands but is typically 40% a.b.v., with EU regulations stipulating a minimum strength of 37.5% a.b.v. (80 proof). Although the majority of vodkas are produced using continuous distillation, a small but growing number use pot stills. Pot still vodkas include Ketel One in the Netherlands, and Tito's and Hangar One in the U.S.A. This inevitably raises the question: which method makes the finest vodka? Both have individual merits and can each produce supreme vodkas. Needless to say, if the resulting vodka doesn't appeal to your palate, then the method used hardly matters.

the fashion for flavors

Flavored vodkas have only recently become fashionable, but this is actually the original style. Distillation methods in Poland and Russia during the 14th and 15th centuries were inevitably crude, and unable to "rectify" (purify) the spirit. The resulting impurities created aggressive odors and flavors, which could only be diminished by infusing the spirit with herbs and spices, while honey tempered its harshness. Once rectification was developed in the mid-19th century, the quality of vodka rose significantly and could be savored without any extras.

The traditional flavoring method means infusing the ingredients, which also results in the flavorings passing on their color. A recent trend for clear liquor has resulted in a host of colorless flavored vodkas. This can be achieved either by using the traditional infusion method then redistilling to remove the color, or by blending colorless aromatic oils with the spirit.

Flavorings can be used very subtly, merely to accentuate the flavor of the grain from which the vodka is distilled. Some apple and fruit distillates are added to Extra Zytnia, for example, which enhance the rye flavor.

Adding flavorings as a "garnish" to the vodka is another approach. Finlandia Lime and Ketel One Citroen, for example, have elegant citrus notes, while the barley and wheat character of each vodka is also readily apparent.

It may seem unlikely that vodka can develop with age, but there is a tradition of aging vodka in oak barrels dating from the 16th century. The Polish and Russian gentry celebrated the birth of a baby by filling empty wine barrels with vodka, to be aged in a cellar until the child's wedding day, when it would provide a toast. Over the years a robust spirit matured into a sophisticated vodka (gaining tannin and "oakey" flavors from the barrel). This tradition continues with Starka (meaning "The Old One").

Originating in Poland and Russia during the Middle Ages, vodka was also established as the national liquor of Scandinavia during the late 16th century. But it was only in the 1950s that the rest of the world began to discover, and produce, vodka—when its mixability made it the ultimate cocktail ingredient. Meanwhile, vodka continues to reign supreme in its original homelands.

where it's made

spirit of the east

Vodka is the national spirit of Poland and Russia, and both countries have always disputed where it originated. There's only circumstantial evidence to support each country's claim, some of which is anecdotal—and entertaining— rather than authoritative.

An undisputed fact is that the knowledge of distillation spread across Europe from Italy and France during the 13th and 14th centuries. It seems likely that distillation reached Poland first, though Russian sources state that delegations from Crimea and Genoa explained the process to a Russian duke in Moscow during the 14th century.

At least the name "vodka" was one thing the Poles and Russians agreed on. However, the debate continues over the origins of the name, with the earliest written reference to vodka appearing on a Polish document dated 1405.

The diminutive form of "*voda*," meaning water, vodka literally means "little water." As water was frequently unsafe to drink during the Middle Ages, "little water" was certainly a more refined option.

Distillation was originally the preserve of the gentry, who produced vodka from grain harvested on their country estates. As these vodkas were sold in local taverns, also owned by the gentry, they enjoyed a lucrative monopoly. Commercial production began to gather momentum during the 16th century, when the merchant classes began to establish distilleries in cities. In Poland these included Cracow, the capital until 1596, Gdansk, the principal seaport, and Lvov (then part of Poland, now part of the Ukraine). The most renowned Russian vodkas were made in Moscow.

As vodka evolved from a medicinal to a social drink during the 16th century, it was embraced by the urban and rural poor. Meanwhile, the merchant classes and the gentry remained faithful to wine, with its "superior" allure and imported status. It wasn't until the 17th century that vodka became a truly egalitarian liquor.

THE EARLIEST VODKAS, INFUSED WITH HERBS AND SPICES, WERE DRUNK ENTIRELY FOR MEDICINAL PURPOSES. THEY WERE ALSO RUBBED ONTO DIFFERENT PARTS OF THE BODY. BELIEVED TO RELIEVE AILMENTS AND PROMOTE LONGEVITY, THESE VODKAS WERE CALLED "ACQUA VITAE," LATIN FOR THE WATER OF LIFE

vodka fit for a tsar

As vodka's popularity began to rise up the social scale during the 17th century, an advocate at the top of the hierarchy was Peter the Great. Succeeding to the Russian throne in 1696, he was not only a keen consumer, but also made a technical contribution to the industry. After a visit to the Netherlands, then at the forefront of distillation technology, the Tsar brought back a greater understanding of the production process. As a result, Russian distillers were able to keep improving the quality of their vodka.

Raising the profile of Russian vodka was Catherine the Great's forte. Crowned Empress in 1762, she sent gifts of vodka to the Swedish and Prussian kings, the French writer Voltaire, and the Swedish botanist and scientist Carl Linnaeus. Not content just to enjoy the vodka, Linnaeus was also inspired to write a treatise entitled *Vodka in the hands of a philosopher, physician, and commoner*.

Later Tsars continued their devoted relationship with the liquor, and in 1886 Tsar Alexander III discovered a vodka that captivated his palate. This happened when Piotr Smirnoff, nephew of Ivan Smirnoff, who founded the Smirnoff company in 1818, served a glass of his vodka to the Tsar. It was a defining moment for Smirnoff vodka, since a royal warrant and extraordinary success followed.

quest for quality

Technical developments continued to raise the quality of vodka during the 18th and 19th centuries. This culminated in the development of continuous distillation and rectification (purification) which resulted in a much purer, mellower spirit from the mid-19th century. Meanwhile, scientists were becoming more involved in distilling, analyzing every aspect of the production process and the ingredients.

Siberia's Sokolovo Distillery, which produces Altai vodka, was established in 1868 by Constantin Platonov. Based in St. Petersburg, he was a specialist in distillation techniques. Platonov believed that water played an important role in the quality of vodka, and his quest for Russia's purest water supply brought him to Sokolovo, in southern Siberia's Altai Mountains. The spring water he discovered there was rich in silver ions, which protected the water from germs and bacteria and were believed to have medicinal benefits.

The Russian chemist, Dmitri Mendeleiev, also made a significant contribution, when he established definitive principles for distilling vodka. These production methods were subsequently ratified as the Tsar's official standard in distilleries.

During the 20th century, state vodka monopolies were established in Poland and Russia, which meant that the government in both countries was directly responsible for quality control. The Russian revolution in 1917 saw the country's distilleries nationalized under the Communist regime, with a state monopoly established in Poland after World War I. When Poland became a satellite of the Soviet Union after World War II, each of its 25 distilleries were nationalized within the Polmos enterprise. Perestroika finally inaugurated a new era for Polish and Russian distilleries, which began to regain their independence in the 1990s.

poland

Almost 50 years of Communist rule in Poland ended with the first democratic elections in 1989, which also heralded a new era for the country's vodka distilleries. The government took an initial step towards privatization in 1991, when each of the 25 Polmos distilleries were granted autonomy—while remaining state-owned.

This new status enabled each Polmos distillery to continue producing the entire range of 49 state-owned vodka brands. This included clear and flavored styles such as Wyborowa, Luksusowa, Cytrynowka, Starka, and Zubrowka.

Meanwhile, autonomy also provided distilleries with exciting new opportunities. Able to negotiate agreements with foreign companies, distilleries were allowed to develop new brands that they owned outright. Numerous new vodkas appeared, ranging from standard brands to deluxe creations such as Belvedere and Chopin.

Deluxe vodkas were a completely new concept in Poland, and had a radically different appearance from state-owned brands, which were packaged in standard-shaped half-liter bottles differentiated only by the label. This new genre established itself with designer packaging, exemplified by Belvedere. Its tall, slim, frosted-glass bottle has a panel of clear

ONCE LIBERATED FROM STATE-
CONTROL IN THE 1990S, POLISH
DISTILLERIES BEGAN LAUNCHING
A HOST OF NEW BRANDS

glass on the front. Looking through this, and the contents, reveals a view of Warsaw's Belvedere Palace.

Although the initial post-Communist euphoria saw many Polish consumers embracing Western brands, particularly Scotch whisky, cognac, and gin, vodka lovers soon realized that Polish brands could offer the same quality and aspirational appeal. This led a major swing back to Polish vodkas, and by the mid 1990s, so many had been launched that there were around 800 to choose from. High-fliers included the Premium range launched by Polmos Poznan and Absolwent from Polmos Bialystok, while Polmos Zyrardow's Belvedere triumphed in the U.S.A.

The next step towards privatization was to assign ownership of each state-owned brand to individual distilleries. This was decided at an auction in 1999, when each Polmos distillery was able to bid for specific brands, such as Wyborowa, Zubrowka, Luksusowa, and Starka. The auction was structured to be as egalitarian as possible, and also to prevent any single distillery from acquiring a monopoly of brands.

Shares in Polmos distilleries were subsequently offered on the international market, with Polish and overseas companies as well as multinationals making bids. The French company Groupe Pernod Ricard, for example, bought a majority shareholding in Polmos Poznan.

A number of privately owned distilleries have also been licensed in Poland, while privately owned brands include the deluxe Potocki vodka launched in 2002. This was created by Jan-Roman Potocki, whose family once owned the Lancut distillery in southeastern Poland.

russia

Perestroika was greeted with great optimism in Russia, and when the vodka industry began to be privatized in 1992, it was seen as a panacea after decades of state ownership. As in Poland, all vodka brands such as Stolichnaya and Moskovskaya were state-owned and produced in various distilleries under license, with excise duty payable on sales. However, once the state monopoly was dismantled, not every distillery paid the duty; some didn't even hold a license.

At one stage, around a hundred licensed distilleries were competing with a few thousand unlicensed operators. Consequently, the character and quality of vodka could vary significantly, depending on its origin. However, the police were generally sympathetic to one front-line retail channel, the *babushkas* (grannies) selling vodka on the streets in an attempt to boost their inadequate incomes.

Moves to reform the situation included lowering tax rates, while also raising fines for non-payment of taxes and producing illicit spirit. The government also established a regulatory body, Rosspirtprom, in 2002, to which it transferred ownership of shares in various distilleries, which remained unsold after trading in shares was suspended in 1998. Modestly priced or even free shares had originally been offered to distillery employees from 1992, with subsequent share offers made available to the public.

During these ongoing reforms, Russian vodkas enjoyed a greater allure following the devaluation of the rouble in 1998. This crisis saw significant price rises in imported vodkas, which had already suffered from the effect of counterfeit "imported" versions (which had delivered variable quality rather than fulfilling consumers' heightened expectations). Consequently, drinking Russian vodka became a way of demonstrating patriotism by the glass.

BEING THE NATIONAL LIQUOR, VODKA IS EAGERLY DISCUSSED AS WELL AS DRUNK BY RUSSIANS, WHO DEBATE THE MERITS OF VARIOUS BRANDS AND DISTILLERIES THAT PRODUCE THEM, WITH SEVERAL HUNDRED VODKAS CURRENTLY ON THE MARKET

Russia's capital, Moscow, is central to the country's vodka industry. A population of 25 million, which includes the largest community of millionaires in Russia, accounts for almost half the country's total vodka consumption. While widespread economic hardship means around 80% of the market is accounted for by economy-priced and standard brands, affluent Muscovites can indulge in a range of deluxe Russian vodkas such as Yuri Dolgoruky. Named after the city's founder, it was launched by the Cristall distillery to celebrate the city's 850th anniversary.

Although hundreds of brands are produced throughout the country, most are regional, with relatively few distributed nationally. As a result many Russians buy from their local distillery. Among the most highly regarded are Moscow's Cristall distillery (established in 1901, and supplier to the Kremlin), Livis in St. Petersburg, Rodnik in

Samara, and the Alkon and Kirishi distilleries in Novgorod, near St. Petersburg. Privately owned distilleries and brands have also been established, including Russky Standart, Stolnaya, Tovaritch, and Flagship.

As Russians are knowledgeable drinkers and actually taste their vodkas, this provides an inherent form of quality control. It also explains why the merits of various vodka brands are a natural talking point. And as advertising hard liquor is prohibited in the country, personal recommendations continue to act as a vital endorsement for every brand.

sweden

The earliest Swedish vodkas, known as *brannvin*, or "burnt wine," were distilled in monasteries and manor houses during the 15th century. Using either wine or grain spirit flavored with herbs and spices, these prototype vodkas served as medicinal remedies. By the late 1500s, brannvin was evolving into a social drink, and during the following century became established as the national drink of Sweden and Finland (which was under Swedish rule from 1150–1809).

The principal grain for producing brannvin was wheat, with potatoes first distilled in Sweden at the end of the 18th century. A key pioneer in the use of potatoes was Countess Eva de la Gardie, who was a scientist as well as an aristocrat. But this was hardly an early example of female emancipation, as distilling was among the list of chores for women on every Swedish farm. Home distilling flourished to such an extent that King Gustav III prohibited this domestic activity in 1775, and established distilleries owned by the Crown instead. However, home distilling continued regardless and the ban was revoked in 1787.

An inspiration to anyone considering a career in the

industry was Lars Olson Smith, "the King of Vodka." Smith's success was preceded by technological innovation, as he introduced continuous distillation to Sweden. This yielded a much purer, mellower spirit, which he launched as Absolut Rent Branvin (Absolute Pure Vodka) in 1879.

At that time, the Utskankningsbolag (an alcoholic beverages monopoly) held the exclusive rights to distil and sell hard liquor in Stockholm. Rather than applying for a retail permit, Smith simply opened a store next to his distillery on the island of Reimersholme, just outside Stockholm and beyond the monopoly's

jurisdiction. Getting there was no problem as Smith provided complimentary boat rides to and from the city. His smooth, higher quality—and less expensive—vodka became a sensation, elevating him to the ranks of Sweden's wealthiest.

Smith was ready to spend, and began acquiring distilleries in Skane. The fertile wheat fields of this southern province meant that so many distilleries were established there that Skane produced more than half of all the liquor distilled in Sweden. Smith's fortunes continued to flourish.

His legacy continues, and a hundred years after the launch of Absolut Rent Branvin, the Swedish alcoholic beverages monopoly, Vin & Sprit, introduced Absolut vodka. Absolut's distinctive packaging was originally inspired by an antique Swedish medicine bottle. Supported by exceptional marketing, Absolut essentially pioneered the premium vodka category in many export markets during the 1980s. Subsequently available in a range of flavors including Kurant, Citron, Peppar, Mandrin, and Vanilla, Absolut became an international sensation.

norway and denmark

Now Norway's most popular hard liquor, vodka took over from the
traditional favorite, akvavit (a grain alcohol flavored with herbs and
spices such as dill and caraway), around 20 years ago. A broad range
of Norwegian vodkas, which are distilled from potatoes, culminate in
deluxe brands such as Christiania.

Vodka has yet to triumph in Denmark, where akvavit maintains its
traditional popularity. However, in 1995, Danish Distillers, the world's
largest producer of akvavit, also began distilling Danzka, a wheat
vodka, followed by flavored variations including Danzka Citron,
Currant, and Grapefruit. The company launched the deluxe wheat
vodka, Fris, in 1997 with a pure, smooth flavor resulting from a unique
"freeze distillation" method.

finland

Finnish vodka began to develop its own individual character during
the 19th century. A major player was the Rajamaki Distillery near
Helsinki, which began distilling vodka in 1889. Within ten years,
Rajamaki had become the largest of Finland's 27 distilleries.

After gaining independence from Russia in 1917 (having been an
autonomous Russian duchy since 1809), Finns soon lost another
freedom. Prohibition—a ban on the production, importation, and sale
of alcohol—was declared in 1919. By 1932, a public referendum
confirmed it was time for a change. While repealing prohibition, the
government nevertheless remained in control of the alcoholic beverages

industry, with Oy Alko established as the state monopoly responsible for producing and retailing alcohol.

Finlandia vodka, the country's most successful brand internationally, was launched in 1970, followed by cranberry- and lime-flavored variations. Meanwhile, the top-selling brand in Finland, Koskenkorva Viina, is a style of vodka that dates from 1953, when Finns had few opportunities to enjoy the liquor other than at home. There were no bars, and drinks and cocktails were only served in restaurants, and accompanied by food. In modest venues, this invariably meant a sandwich, which had to be present on the table before the drink was served. This frequently unwanted, uneaten sandwich would subsequently be "sold" to the next customer ordering alcohol. Occasionally the kitchen received an alarm call: "Someone's eaten the sandwich!" and a replacement had to be prepared.

Another great favorite in Finland is Koskenkorva Salmiakki (technically a flavored vodka liqueur), which became a phenomenon after its launch in 1992. It was destined for success. Salmiakki (salty black licorice) is Finland's most popular confectionery, and this liquid version yields a luscious, lightly salty, black licorice flavor with minty anise and chocolate hints.

Finland's entry into the E.U. in 1995 ended the state monopoly on producing vodka and other alcoholic drinks. Consequently, privately owned companies introduced new brands such as Savon Wiinaa and Pramia. Meanwhile, the state retail monopoly, Alko, continues, with Alko's limited opening hours inspiring a classic Finnish phrase; "the Friday bottle;" bought for the weekend, since until 1991, Alko stores were closed on Saturdays.

vodka goes west

As the world's most fashionable liquor, vodka has also become one of the most widely produced. Following the current vodka trail can easily take your palate on a round-the-world trip, from Iceland to Mongolia and New Zealand, via Ireland, Belgium, Germany, and Italy; and from Canada to Brazil, through the U.S.A., Mexico, and the Caribbean. This roll-call beyond vodka's traditional homelands includes many innovative brands.

As Europe's leading vodka market, the U.K. gets through six million cases per year. The British taste for vodka was essentially created by Smirnoff, which has dominated the U.K. scene ever since it was launched in 1952. Meanwhile, the range of British vodkas is diversifying. This includes Utkins U.K.5, which has been distilled from organic rye since 1999. Making its debut in 2002, Graffiti is a wheat vodka that includes malted barley. This is a rarity as virtually all vodkas use commercially produced enzymes instead of malted barley to help convert starches into sugar during the production process.

Among the vodkas enjoying celebrity status in the U.K. and U.S.A. is the Dutch brand Ketel One, launched in 1992, with Ketel One Citroen following in 2000. Produced at the Nolet distillery in Schiedam, Ketel One is distilled using traditional copper pot stills (*ketel* is Dutch for still), which is the most historic method. The distillery itself is equally historic, and has been owned by the Nolet family ever since it was established in 1691.

Another eminent resident of Schiedam is the Dirkzwager distillery, family-owned since 1891, which also promotes a fellow Dutch institution by producing Vincent van Gogh vodka. With each style of vodka featuring different Van Gogh paintings on the bottle, these truly are works of art.

France has an illustrious tradition of distilling hard liquor, but not vodka. Nevertheless, it was in the Cognac region that the concept for the ultra-premium Grey Goose was created. Distilling grains as a break from grapes led to the idea of blending the distillates (blending is a standard practice when producing cognac). And so Grey Goose was conceived as a blend of corn, wheat, rye, and barley, with the local Genté springs providing the water. Launched in the U.S.A. in 1997, Grey Goose soon attained cult status followed by flavored variations, L'Orange and Le Citron.

u.s.a.

As the world's second largest vodka market after Russia, the U.S.A. is a target destination for vodkas from around the globe. In fact, sales of imported vodkas are accelerating in the U.S.A., with this status acting as a "guarantee" of quality, not to mention fulfilling lifestyle aspirations.

The U.S.A. essentially discovered vodka in the 1950s, when Smirnoff's eminent mixability became a phenomenon. The early years in America, however, weren't an easy ride. Nor was the vodka's journey to the U.S.A. Following the Russian Revolution in 1917, the Smirnoff distillery was nationalized and the owner, Vladimir Smirnoff, sentenced to death. However, White Russian forces stormed the Piatigorsk prison before the sentence was carried out, allowing him to escape to Poland and then France. All he took with him was the Smirnoff name and the recipe.

Trying to establish Smirnoff vodka in Paris proved difficult, leading Vladimir into an agreement with another Russian émigré, Rudolf Kunett. When prohibition was repealed in the U.S.A., Kunett acquired the rights to sell Smirnoff vodka under license in America from Vladimir. Kunett's American Dream didn't really come true, and in 1937 he sold out to an alcoholic beverages company, Heublein.

Everything changed when Smirnoff became the basis for a new cocktail, the Moscow Mule (Smirnoff mixed with ginger ale and lime juice). This was immediately hailed as a modern classic, and Smirnoff became the archetypal vodka for mixing cocktails.

While traditional vodkas continue to dominate the market, a new generation of specialty brands has recently added a new perspective. California, for example, is home to some innovative deluxe vodkas. Charbay, in Napa Valley, began by launching a range of flavored vodkas in 1997. These include Blood Orange and Meyer Lemon, as well as Ruby Red Grapefruit and Key Lime.

Hangar One, produced in St. George, California, is a pot-still vodka which is also available in a range of flavors. Buddha's Hand Citron is flavored with a particular variety of the citrus family, and other fruit flavors include Kaffir Lime and Mandarin Blossom.

Heading east, Tito's vodka hails from the Mockingbird distillery, the first and only licensed distillery in Texas. Created by Tito Beveridge, this pot-still vodka is distilled from corn, while organic grain is behind Rain vodka, distilled in Kentucky. Meanwhile, potato vodkas are also appearing with Idaho potatoes being the basis of Teton Glacier and Zodiac.

Vodka plays an essential role in the social life of Eastern Europe and Scandinavia, and numerous occasions are celebrated with a glass of the national liquor. How vodka is drunk, and the food that accompanies it, varies according to where it's being served. Poland, Russia, Sweden, and Finland each have their own customs and preferences, which account for an individual "vodka culture" in each country.

enjoying vodka

sip or shoot

Russians have a history of shooting rather than sipping their vodka. This is based on a traditional belief that the fumes, rather than the liquid, were to blame for inducing a state of intoxication. Consequently, downing in one was a cunning ruse to prevent fumes from trespassing up the nasal passages, meaning a vodka "session" could, in theory at least, continue for that much longer.

Sipping is the best way to savor vodka, and Poles sip as much as shoot. It is also traditional in Poland to serve vodka at room temperature. The origins of this custom are entirely practical, as it predates refrigeration. However, chilling promotes a vodka's dominant characteristics while diminishing subtler nuances, so more complex vodkas—particularly flavored styles—reveal their credentials more readily at room temperature.

During a vodka session in Poland or Russia there's no debate about whether to shoot or sip, as the host decides which method should be used. It's also customary to vary the approach during a session, and when raising a glass the host indicates what should be done by repeating either "*do dna*" ("to the bottom"), or "*ciut, cuit*" ("bit by bit").

Another popular Russian custom is to serve vodka with a separate glass of water or fruit juice on the side. Moreover, a classic Russian saying, "beer without vodka is like throwing money away," shows that vodka needn't be excluded when beer is served either.

TRADITIONALLY IN RUSSIA AND POLAND IT IS THE HOST WHO ANNOUNCES WHETHER TO SIP OR SHOOT WITH THE WORDS: *"CUIT, CUIT"* OR *"DO, DNA"*

toasts and traditions

The usual Polish and Russian toast, "*na zdrowie*" or "*na zdorovye*" ("to your health") is only one of many. A new job, car, coat—or in fact anything deemed appropriate—provides an opportunity for Poles to say "*to trzeba oblac*" (literally, "it needs to be wetted"), and down a celebratory glass. Another Polish saying that justifies the next round of vodka is "*chlusniem bo usniem.*" This means "let's down another one, or we'll fall asleep," which unfortunately doesn't rhyme when translated.

A Russian vodka session actually evolves through a series of toasts, as vodka is only drunk after proposing a toast. Another popular rule is that the pause between the first and second toast should be as brief as possible. The host typically opens with "*so svidaniyem*" ("nice to see you again") or "*za droujbou*" ("to friendship"), with the final toast of the evening being "*na passachok*" ("before leaving").

Once a glass has been drained, a Russian superstition states that smashing it on the floor promotes good fortune. This operates on a simple sliding scale—the more glasses smashed, the luckier you become.

scandinavian style

Scandinavians usually mix vodka with soft drinks and juices. Drinking neat vodka, known as *snaps*, is restricted to specific occasions such as Christmas, Labor Day, Midsummer's Night, and crayfish parties.

In Finland, a formal toast entails raising a glass by holding the arm so that it's horizontal from the shoulder to the elbow. For Swedes, the correct height at which to hold a glass for a toast is level with the third shirt button. Politeness requires direct eye contact with each person in the drinking circle and after downing the vodka this is repeated, accompanied by a small nod.

The usual Finnish toast is "*kippis*," and the Swedish toast is "*skal*" ("cheers"). These can also extend into a drinking song, followed by a shot of vodka downed in one. "Helan Gar" is the title of a rousing song popular in both countries. The lyrics refer to the formal tradition of each guest having two glasses of *snaps*, one filled to the brim and the second half-full. Anyone who doesn't drink the full glass down in one forfeits the right to the half-glass (which is firm, but fair).

food

"*Vodka is only drunk for a reason, and if you have a bottle of vodka you'll always find a reason*", is a classic Russian saying. A great reason for a session is that Poles and Russians always serve food with vodka, creating an instant party. This doesn't mean assembling a plate of whatever's handy, simply to act as ballast for the alcohol. A traditional range of specialties, known as "*zakuski*" in Russian and "*zakaski*" in Polish, is served. Although this literally means "a nibble," the usual selection can keep you going all evening. A star turn is caviar and blinis with sour cream, though at an everyday session a blini is more likely to bear lox or salted herring fillets. A ubiquitous staple, salted herrings arrive at the table in various guises. One popular Russian dish is "herring under a fur coat." The fur coat in question is a layer of grated, cooked beets and slices of hard-boiled egg in mayonnaise. Other favorites include pickled cucumbers and mushrooms, spicy sausages and charcuterie, curd cheese, and rye bread.

Swedish and Finnish favorites served with vodka include salted fish roe and gravadlax. Late-night vodka sessions in Finland are also sustained by *vorschmak* (a lamb, salted herring, anchovy, onion, and sour cream casserole) and Jansson's Temptation (potatoes, anchovies, and cream).

An annual highlight for Swedes and Finns are the crayfish parties held during a season that lasts from early August to mid-October. The menu features crayfish cooked with dill and salt, served with toast and fresh dill. Finnish tradition dictates that each time the claws of a crayfish are detached a glass of vodka is downed in one.

In Sweden, partygoers dress for the occasion, wearing small cone-shaped hats and bibs decorated with crayfish. The theme even extends to bunting and lanterns. Tradition stipulates that men focus their attention on the female to their right, who is known as the *bordsdam* (table lady). Some hosts prefer to serve *vasterboten ost* (cheese) and toast before the crayfish, others reverse the order. Either way, after every drinking song, a glass of *snaps* goes down in one, and every time *snaps* is drunk a song is sung.

While the rest of Sweden throws crayfish parties, August sees eel parties held on the beaches of the south coast, ideally in a cottage or fisherman's hut. Dinner features eel prepared in various ways, and traditionally the party goes on all night. It's still considered poor manners to leave before morning, and there's plenty of vodka or akvavit (grain spirit flavored with various herbs and spices) available. Another bonus is that whoever collects the most eel bones around the edge of their plate is proclaimed eel king or queen.

Apart from being classics in their own right, the specialties served in Scandinavia and Eastern Europe have a genuine rapport with vodka. Rich flavors stand up to the full-bodied nature of the vodka, which makes a contribution in return. Salted herring fillets, for example, become meatier and less salty under the influence of vodka, while sour cream tastes wonderfully molten. Spicy, salty flavors create a natural demand for the next round of vodka, which then prompts more food, and they continue to perpetuate each other. It's the perfect relationship.

sing song

Guava adds a tropical touch to this cocktail, which balances the refreshing acidity of lime juice with simple syrup.

2 oz. vodka

1 oz. lime juice

½ oz. simple syrup

guava juice

lemon and lime slices, to garnish

Combine the first three ingredients in a tall glass with ice, top up with guava juice and garnish with the lemon and lime slices.

tatanka

A contemporary classic in Poland, where cocktail culture is only just beginning to take off, this is a new way to drink a historic favorite.

1–2 oz. Zubrowka (Bison) vodka

apple juice

lemon wedge, to garnish

Pour the vodka into a tall glass with ice (optional) and top up with apple juice. Garnish with a lemon wedge.

the dry martini

The world's ultimate cocktail,
with a mystique that no other classic
cocktail can match.

½ oz. dry vermouth

3 oz. vodka

an olive or a lemon twist,
   to garnish

Stir both the ingredients in a
mixing glass filled with ice and
strain into a martini glass.
Garnish with an olive or a
lemon twist.

cosmopolitan

Emerging in the U.S.A. during the
1990s, this cocktail has already joined
the ranks of "modern classic cocktails"
and is definitely here to stay.

1½ oz. lemon vodka

¾ oz. Cointreau

¾ oz. cranberry juice

a dash of lime juice, lime
   cordial, and orange bitters

orange zest, to garnish

Shake the ingredients in a cocktail
shaker three-quarters full of ice
and strain into a martini glass.
Heat a piece of orange zest briefly
with the flame of a lighter, then
squeeze out the essential oils onto
the surface of the cocktail.
Garnish with the zest.

gothic martini

Rather than appearing in jams, jellies,
or fruit crumbles, blackberries are
given an ultimate purpose in this
fruity concoction.

2 oz. vodka

a dash of crème de mure

a dash of Sambuca

6 blackberries, (2 to garnish)

Add all the ingredients to a cocktail
shaker three-quarters full of ice, shake
sharply and strain into a martini glass.
Garnish with two blackberries.

the twinkle

Combining vodka with another
ultimate indulgence, champagne, and
the enigmatic flavor of elderflower
gives a sparkling result.

2 oz. vodka

1 oz. champagne

a dash elderflower cordial

lemon peel, to garnish

Stir the ingredients over ice
in a mixing glass, then strain
into a martini glass and garnish
with a twist of lemon.

credits

Aria

133 & 295–296 Upper Street

Islington

London N1 2TU

t. +44 (0)20 7704 6222

www.ariashop.co.uk

Baltic

(Eastern European Restaurant

& Vodka Bar)

74 Blackfriars Road

London SE1 8HA

t. +44 (0)20 7928 1111

f. +44 (0)20 7928 8487

www.balticrestaurant.co.uk

Caviar House

La Boutique

Shop & Café Nikolaj

161 Piccadilly

London W1V 9DF

t. +44 (0)20 7409 0445

www.caviar-house.com

Flin Flon

138 St John Street

London EC1V 4UA

t. +44 (0)20 7253 8849

www.flinflon.co.uk

Origin Modernism

25 Camden Passage

London N1 8EA

t. +44 (0)20 7704 1326

www.origin101.co.uk

Purple Bar, Sanderson Hotel

50 Berners Street

London W1P 4AD

t. +44 (0)20 7300 1496

www.ianschragerhotels.com

Revolution Bar

St Anne's Court

Soho

London W1F 0AZ

t. +44 (0)20 7434 0330

www.revolution-bars.co.uk

All photography by **William Lingwood**, (unless otherwise stated)

14 left, 18 & 18–19 ã **2003 V&S VIN & SPRIT AB**

14 right **Chris Tubbs**

15 right **Francesca Yorke**

16–17,19, 22 right **Finlandia Vodka**

22 left © **Nolet Distillery Schiedam-Holland www.KetelOne.com**

(InSpirit Brands t. 020 7377 9457)

23 left & 42 © **Ian Wisniewski**

index

A
Absolut 39, 17
aging vodka 20
alcohol strength 17, 18, 19
Alexander III, Tsar 26
Alko 42
Alkon 37
Altai 11, 29

B
barley 11, 17, 45
Belvedere 32, 33
blended vodkas 11
brands 10
brannvin 38
Britain 45
Buddha's Hand Citron 46

C
Catherine the Great, Empress 26
Chopin 32
Christiania 41
cocktails 9, 58–61
continuous stills 18–19, 29, 39
corn 11, 17
Cosmopolitan 9, 59
Cracow 25
Cristall 37
Cytrynowka 13, 30

D
Danzka 13, 41
deluxe vodkas 32, 46
Denmark 41
Dirkzwager distillery 45
distillation 18–19, 20, 25, 29
Dry Martini 9, 59

E
Estonia 17
Extra Zytnia 20

F
Finland 11, 17, 38, 41–2, 53, 55–6
Finlandia 11, 17, 20, 42
Flagship 37
flavors 11–13, 20, 46
food, serving with vodka 55–6
France 45, 46
fruit-flavored vodka 13

G
Gdansk 25
glasses, smashing 52
Gothic Martini 60
Graffiti 45
grain 11, 17, 18
Grey Goose 11, 13, 45
Groupe Pernod Ricard 33
Gustav III, King of Sweden 38

H
Hangar One 19, 46
herbs 13
history 25–9

I
ingredients 17

K
Ketel One 13, 19, 20, 45
Kirishi 37
Koskenkorva 17, 42
Kremlyovskaya Chocolate 13
Krupnik 13

L
la Gardie, Countess Eva de 38
lemon-flavored vodka 13
Limonnaya 13
Linnaeus, Carl 26
Livis 37
Luksusowa 30, 33
Lvov 25

M
Martini 9, 59, 60
Mendeleiev, Dmitri 29
mixers 53
Moscow 25, 37
Moscow Mule 9, 46
Moskovskaya 34

N
Netherlands 13, 19, 26, 45
Norway 17, 41

P
Pertsovka 13
Peter the Great, Tsar 26
Pieprzowka 13
Platonov, Constantin 29
Poland 11, 13, 17, 20, 25, 29, 30–3, 51, 52, 55
Polmos 33, 30
Polstar Cucumber 13
pot stills 18–19
potato vodkas 17, 38, 41, 46
Potocki 11, 33

R
Rain vodka 46
Rajamaki Distillery 41
rectification 20, 29
Rodnik 37
Russia 11, 13, 20, 25–9, 34–7, 46, 51, 52, 55
Russky Standart 11, 37
rye 11, 17

S
Scandinavia 53, 56
shooting vodka 51
Siberia 17
Sing Song 58
sipping vodka 51
Smirnoff 26, 45, 46
Smith, Lars Olson 39

Sokolovo Distillery 29
Starka 20, 33
stills 18–19
Stolichnaya 13, 34
Stolnaya 37
Sweden 11, 17, 38–9, 53, 55, 56

T
Tatanka 58
temperature, serving 51
Teton Glacier 46
Tito's 19, 46
toasts 52, 53
Tovaritch 37
The Twinkle 61

U
United States 11, 17, 19, 45, 46
Utkins U.K.5 45

V
Vincent van Gogh vodka 45

W
water 29
wheat 11, 17, 38
Wyborowa 11, 13, 30, 33

Y
yeast 18
Yuri Dolgoruky 37

Z
Zodiac 46
Zoladkowa Gorzka 13
Zoladkowka 13
Zubrowka 13, 30, 33

acknowledgments

Special thanks to Tony Conigliaro, cocktail maestro, for providing the recipes.

I would also like to thank: Tarja Tuunanen, Markku Raittinen, and Leena Poukka of Finlandia vodka, Markku Maki and Juha Kahima of Primalco, Sirpa Tuunanen from Finlandia House, Ulrika Lovdahl and the Absolut Akademi at Absolut Vodka, Henriette Holmgreen from Danish Distillers, Katarzyna Plonska from Agros, Oscar Holm of Polstar Vodka, Richard Storer from Grey Goose, Przemyslaw Zielinksi and Armando Simoes da Silva of Knightsbridge Portfolio Services, Jan-Roman Potocki from Potocki Vodka, Bob Nolet from Ketel One, James Shelbourne and Stuart Ekins from InSpirit brands, Chris Parker of the Organic Spirits Company, and The Wine & Spirit Historical Museum of Stockholm.